GLOBAL QUESTIONS

Is the Media Too Powerful?

GLOBAL QUESTIONS

Is the Media Too Powerful?

David Abbott

ARCTURUS

This edition first published in 2010 by Arcturus Publishing
Distributed by Black Rabbit Books
P.O. Box 3263
Mankato
Minnesota MN 56002

Printed in the United States

Series concept: Alex Woolf
Editors: Jonathan Hilton and Karen Taschek
Designer: Ian Winton
Picture researcher: Jonathan Hilton

Library of Congress Cataloging-in-Publication Data

Abbott, David.
  Is the media too powerful? / by David Abbott.
      p. cm. -- (Global questions)
  Includes index.
  Summary: "This series takes an in-depth look at some of the major issues and crises that are on the front pages of today's newspapers. Each book looks at the historical background to the questions and offers balanced reporting of the situation and several solutions to the problem. Features include timelines, maps and primary sources"--Provided by publisher.
  ISBN 978-1-84837-685-4 (library binding)
  1. Mass media--Juvenile literature. 2. Press--Juvenile literature. I. Title.
  P91.2.A23 2011
  302.23--dc22
                                    2010011025

Picture credits:
Corbis: Cover (Christophe D'Yvoire/Sygma), title page (Najlah Feanny), 6 (Bettmann), 7 (Sion Touhig), 8 (Bettmann), 9 (Jacques Langevin/Sygma), 10 (Lorenzo Ciniglio/Sygma), 11 (Alessandra Benedetti), 12 (Matthew Cavanaugh/epa), 14 (Bettmann), 16 (Reuters TV/Reuters), 17 (Omar Sobhani/Reuters), 18 (Bettmann), 19 (Rick Wilking/Reuters), 20 (Mark E Gibson), 21 (Rick Maiman/Sygma), 22 (Bettmann), 23 (Antoine Serra/In Visu), 24 (James Leynse), 25 (Matthew Cavanaugh/ epa), 26 (Sygma), 27 (Bettmann), 28 (Robert Ghement/epa), 29 (Liu Liqun), 30 (Everett Kennedy Brown/epa), 33 (Lucy Nicholson/Reuters), 34 (Andy Rain/epa), 35 (Seth Wenig/Reuters), 36 (Reuters), 37 (James Leynse), 38 (Ym Yik/epa), 40 (Chad Hunt), 41 (Gavin Hellier/JAI), 42 (Dennis Van Tine/Retna Ltd), 43 (Christian Charisius/Reuters).
Getty Images: 31 (AFP).
Press Association Images: 15 (Eddie Adams/AP), 39 (Evert Elzinga/AP).

Cover caption: The press pack waits, cameras poised, for the stars' arrival at the Academy Awards ceremony.
Title page caption: A modern, state-of-the-art television console gives producers the power to manipulate and edit the images that are transmitted to viewers all around the world.

SL001355US   Supplier 02 Date 0510

Contents

Chapter 1:   What is the media?   6

Chapter 2:   How powerful is the media?   12

Chapter 3:   How does the media influence us?   18

Chapter 4:   Does the media protect our freedom?   24

Chapter 5:   How is the media regulated?   32

Chapter 6:   How is the media changing?   38

Glossary   44

Further information   45

Index   46

What is the media?

To understand how important the media is, just think how much it figures in your daily life. Turning on the TV or radio is probably one of the first things you do each day. More than likely, you spend a few hours a day watching TV, and you are also probably spending more and more of your time e-mailing, texting, or surfing the Internet. People say they cannot survive without their TV or Internet connection, so is the media too powerful? Does it have too much influence on us as individuals and on society at large?

The word *media* is used mainly to describe newspapers and television and radio stations. But *mass media* refers to any technologies, designed to communicate to a mass audience. So the Internet, books, blogs, Twitter, and podcasts all count as mass media, as do cell phones, movies, and video games.

Expert View

Marshall McLuhan (1911–1980), a Canadian writer on media theory, thought that the media had an unwelcome influence on modern society, shaping every aspect of our lives and identities:

"Any technology tends to create a new human environment . . . Technological environments are not merely passive containers of people but are active processes that reshape people and other technologies alike."

Marshall McLuhan, **The Gutenberg Galaxy**

McLuhan is famous for the idea that electronic communications have turned the world into a global village. Electronic technology makes communication so fast that news and ideas are easily accessible to everyone, all over the world.

Modern technology means that news channels and papers can be produced and accessed anywhere in the world. This also means that the media is a global business. Media organizations, such as the Al Jazeera network in the Middle East, compete internationally for readers and viewers—and for news.

Do we control the media . . . ?

Different societies have different ways of controlling the mass media. In what are generally considered democratic societies, it is claimed that there is a free press and freedom of speech: journalists and news organizations can publish what they want as long as they obey the laws designed to protect individuals from false accusations. In democracies, politicians try to avoid interfering in the running of the media, and control of media organizations is usually on a voluntary basis.

In more authoritarian regimes, where regular elections might be rare, the media is often run by the state. Critics and observers of such societies claim that political pressure, the law, and sometimes physical force are all used to control what is published. In such societies, the press is not free, and what is published is strongly censored.

. . . Or does the media control us?

Media analysts, including Canadian Marshall McLuhan, have argued that the media—in whatever kind of society—is in reality more powerful than this picture suggests. McLuhan claimed that modern media, such as newspapers and the Internet, in fact make us think and act automatically in certain ways and so have a more powerful effect on us than most people believe.

The rise of the media

In order to understand how the media came to be such a powerful force in modern society, you need to know a little of its history. Before the invention of the first movable-type printing press by Johannes Gutenberg in the 1440s, producing books and other reading material was slow, laborious, and expensive. Although strictly speaking, books have always been a form of mass media, before the 1440s the primitive printing technology, high cost, and low literacy rates meant that they were read by very few people.

Growth of the mass media	
1440s	Gutenberg Press
1702	*Daily Courant*
1920s	First radio stations in US
1925	John Logie Baird transmits first television signals
1928	Television broadcasts start in US
1938	Orson Welles broadcasts *The War of the Worlds* and panics America (see page 18)
1949	Network television starts in the US
1954	NBC makes first coast-to-coast color broadcast
1967	First color broadcasts on BBC2
1972	In the US, color TVs outnumber black and white
1990	Satellite broadcasting starts
1990	Internet access for public use

After the invention of the mechanical printing press, books could be reproduced in great numbers and at a much lower cost. As technology developed and more and more people learned to read and write, the market for books increased over time, and a new market for newspapers developed. This was particularly true in European and other Western societies in the eighteenth century as they industrialized and became more prosperous. The audience for books and newspapers became a truly mass one: it was possible for many people to read the same material.

Coffeehouses and taverns in eighteenth-century London gave the first journalists a place to drink and gossip. Times have changed, but journalism works in a similar way today: top journalists still need to meet with politicians, businesspeople, and civil servants, and they still like to meet in comfortable surroundings.

Modern politicians have to be consummate media performers. Being able to handle the media circus is a large part of any politician's job, and managing the media is a crucial means of influencing public opinion. As French politician Marie-George Buffet demonstrates, a key skill is the ability to remain calm in the midst of a media frenzy.

Modern society and public opinion

It was in the eighteenth century that a truly mass media was created and what we now call "public opinion" was formed. German media expert Jürgen Habermas (born 1929) says that this first developed in Britain, where London coffeehouses came to be places where the new social elite—businessmen, journalists, and politicians—started to argue and swap opinions on the issues of the day. This socially privileged café society soon needed other forms of communication, and one of the first daily papers in Britain established to satisfy this need was the *Daily Courant*, published in 1702 in Fleet Street. This new elite and the early newspapers quickly became an important social force.

However, experts such as Jürgen Habermas and American sociologist C. Wright Mills (1916–1962) have argued that the creation of the mass media has not led to a more democratic society. On the contrary, what the new mass media has done from the beginning of the eighteenth century is to create a force that reflects the interests of elite social groups and that manages and controls public opinion.

Expert View

American sociologist C. Wright Mills has argued that the development of a mass media in modern society does not necessarily mean that the public is better informed:

"With the increased means of mass persuasion that are available, the public has become the object of intensive efforts to control, manage, manipulate, and increasingly intimidate [it]."

C. Wright Mills, **The Power Elite**

Media ownership

Many of those who argue that the media is too powerful point to the fact that it is controlled by a small number of owners. In the US about 10 corporations dominate media ownership. In the UK, four companies account for 85 percent of national daily and Sunday newspapers. Increasingly, these big companies are multinational. News Corporation, for example, owned by Rupert Murdoch, operates News International, which owns many newspapers in the UK—*The Times*, *The Sunday Times*, *Times Supplements*, *The Sun*, and *News of the World*. News Corporation is a conglomerate—a company that itself owns many other companies—and those companies in turn own many newspapers, publishing companies, TV and radio

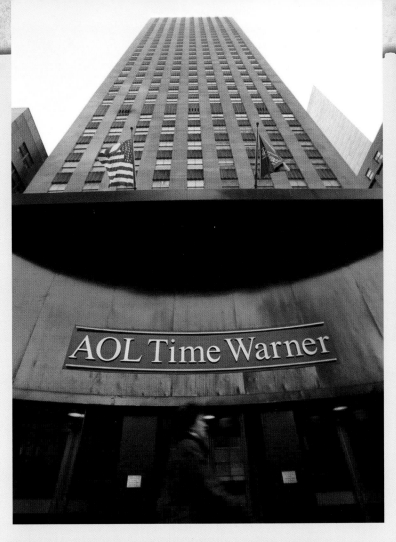

AOL Time Warner is the one of the world's largest conglomerates and owns famous TV channels such as HBO and CNN and magazines such as *Marie Claire*. The company is led by its chairman, the relatively low-profile Jeffrey Bewkes, who earns around $19 million a year.

stations, and other holdings in the UK, US, Australia and the Pacific Islands. There are other significant media players, such as Sony, Bertelsmann AG, Viacom, and Time Warner, but it is still a case of a few big corporations dominating the market.

Why it matters

Those who argue that the media is too powerful claim that big corporations and rich owners can have too much influence on which stories the media selects to report and how it reports them. For example, critics of Rupert Murdoch argue that his UK newspapers are frequently critical of the BBC. The domination of the media by a few large companies, argue some, means that reporting inevitably provides only a narrow range of views for the public to think about.

Opinions can differ widely concerning the integrity of media moguls:

Ted Turner, founder of CNN, a rival network to Rupert Murdoch's Fox News, criticized Fox, saying that it was producing "propaganda" in support of President Bush in 2005: "Just because you're bigger doesn't mean you're right."

Ted Turner, in a speech to television executives

"Murdoch's achievement is that he is the only media mogul to have created and to control a truly global media empire. He understood sooner than anyone else the opportunities offered by new technology to create first an international press and then a television domain."

William Shawcross, Time *magazine, 1999*

What's your opinion?

Running a media organization requires a lot of money, and big companies are able to drive down their costs and sell products cheaply in order to beat off the competition. But the importance of generating large advertising revenues can lead to conflicts of interest.

The end result, say critics, is lazy journalism that fears to criticize the business community. Another outcome, it is argued, is that the media produces what sells best—tabloid newspapers with short, sensationalist articles and pictures of celebrities and naked women.

These claims are controversial and can be hard to prove. But what seems clear is that wider media ownership can make for a media industry that better reflects the range of public opinions.

Silvio Berlusconi's media empire started with a cable TV company and expanded into a local TV network and then into one of Italy's largest publishing houses. He is alleged to have had control of 90 percent of Italian TV when he became prime minister in 2001.

Chapter 2

How powerful is the media?

Those who argue that the media is vital to democracy would say that the media needs to be powerful in order to hold politicians to account. But can politicians and officials manipulate the media?

Politicians and the media

A positive media image is becoming increasingly necessary if politicians are to be successful in modern public life. For that reason, it is now commonplace for politicians

President Barack Obama fields questions at a press conference. There is tremendous competition among the press corps since posing good questions enhances a journalist's reputation.

to hire public relations experts, or spin doctors, to help them try to improve their media presentation skills and to attempt to manipulate news stories that are reported or broadcast about them or their policies.

Politicians can shape news stories in a number of ways. In interviews, they can avoid answering questions directly, divert attention to what their political opponents are doing or saying, or give confusing, overlong, overcomplicated answers. Politicians can also make comments to journalists "off the record," perhaps passing on information or rumors critical of their opponents. Another tactic is to release unflattering news about themselves when some other major story is dominating the airwaves—this makes it more likely that the bad news will get less attention or, possibly, not even be reported. And politicians can simply refuse to speak to certain journalists. Journalists need information, so if a politician will not speak to them or goes to a rival journalist, they may find themselves with nothing to report. This means journalists have to be careful what they say—a form of self-censorship.

Tricks of the trade

The media plays an important role in shaping what gets debated and how politicians are portrayed, but politicians play an active role in this process. Public debates are a good example of this and have been a feature of the US presidential election system since 1988. Part of the skill is to remain calm, but using "dog-whistle politics" or other types of negative campaigning is also effective. Like a dog whistle, only those sensitive to a certain frequency will pick up on the hidden meaning, making it easy to deny. In the 2008 presidential election, unsuccessful candidate Senator John McCain was accused by some critics of trying to appeal to voters' racism while keeping his comments vague enough to make any denials plausible.

Expert View

"Since news is increasingly framed to parallel (and compete with) entertainment shows, or sports events, so is its logic. It requires drama, suspense, conflict, rivalries, greed, deception, winners and losers, and, if possible, sex and violence. Following the pace, and language, of sports casting, 'horse race politics' is reported as an endless game of ambitions, maneuvers, strategies, and counter-strategies, with the help of insider confidences and constant opinion polling from the media themselves."

Professor Manuel Castells, **The Information Age,** *Vol. II*

The first casualty

It is often said that the first casualty of war is the truth. When journalists report on a conflict that their own country is involved in, it can be hard for them to avoid bias, no matter how good their training has been. Imagine if your own country was losing a war: you might be tempted to downplay heavy defeats and casualties, or you might be suspicious about enemy claims of success. And even if journalists are reporting a war their own country is not involved in, they might well have sympathies for one side, leading to biased reporting.

The media's role in war

The role of the media becomes ambiguous in wartime—should it report the truth without fear or favor, whatever the consequences, or should the media unabashedly provide moral support for its own side? For governments and the military, the effect of press coverage might jeopardize war aims, and not just by giving away military information. In the case of the Vietnam War (1961–1975), for example, it has been argued that TV reports showing the horrific sight of piles of American body bags turned public opinion against the war. Another point of view is that democratic governments can mislead their people and so need to be questioned at all times, but especially during war.

American body bags being loaded onto a helicopter at the height of the Vietnam War (1961–1975). Since Vietnam, the media in some countries has not shown so much of the reality of war. The public in the UK and the US, for example, have seen few images of death from Iraq and Afghanistan.

Eddie Adams's iconic photograph of General Loan executing a Vietcong fighter in Saigon revealed the brutality of the Vietnam War to millions. What is the role of the media in war?

Embedded reporters

As technology has advanced and the media has come to play a greater role in all areas of modern life, governments and the military in many societies have had to keep pace with increased demands from the public for news and information. In many countries, the military has introduced the idea of "embedded reporters"—reporters who are attached to and supervised by military units—as a way of providing news stories. Critics, however, point to the potential problems of such a close relationship between media and military, arguing that journalists attached to the military might become more sympathetic to a military viewpoint and will certainly have less freedom to move around and find the most truthful or revealing stories.

Expert View

Former BBC reporter Martin Bell gives this insight into the realities of being a war reporter during the Bosnia war in the 1990s:

"We do self-censor . . . There are things we cannot show; nearly all the TV pictures of the mortar bombing of the marketplace in Sarajevo, and the scenes in a cellar in Ahmici where a Muslim family of seven, including mother, grandparents, and children, were burned to death by the Croats. Television often stands accused of exaggerating the events it relates and wrenching them out of context, but in Bosnia it consistently understated the facts where it did know them and under-reported them where it didn't."

Martin Bell, **In Harm's Way**

Reporting terrorism

Some people's first thought on the issue of how the media reports terrorism is that terrorism can be treated in just the same way as war. But this assumes that terrorism is easy to define and understand. With this approach, the only problems arising for the media would be whether they are biased—for or against—the terrorists, whether graphic images of violence should be shown, and what the media can do to ensure that information that could endanger the public or the security forces is not published.

But this approach fails to understand what terrorism is and how it works. There are many different types of terrorism, but one central element is that terrorism involves the use of violence for political purposes: political violence. By using violence against civilians, terrorists aim to create panic and

Television producers have to make difficult decisions about how to treat images such as this, showing Hamas gunmen displaying remains of Israeli soldiers. If they do not publish such images, they could be seen as failing to do their job as reporters and the public will be misinformed as a result.

fear and to intimidate leaders in order to force political change. This is a strategy highly dependent on the mass media, for without it, it can be argued, terrorist acts would be far less effective. For the media, therefore, terrorism poses one dilemma that arguably occurs only occasionally in war: should they publicize and report acts of terrorism, or does that provide only what is sometimes called the "oxygen of publicity" to terrorists?

Can we trust the professionals?

Many media professionals might argue that this problem is not really a dilemma at all. It is certainly a challenge, but many journalists would be of the opinion that their training and professional judgment enable them to strike a balance between unintentionally glamorizing or justifying acts of terrorism and reporting it responsibly to a public that needs to know the truth.

FORUM

People can use the same word to mean very different things:

"... One person's terrorist may be another person's freedom fighter, and there are former 'terrorists' holding elected office in many parts of the world."

Guardian *newspaper style guide*

"There are broad principles, some enshrined in historic discussions, some in international law, including the Geneva conventions, which limit the violence that dissidents and states can legitimately use. These principles take terrorism out of the realm of the subjective: one person's terrorist is not another's freedom fighter."

Fred Halliday, Two Hours That Shook the World

What's your opinion?

Others, though, would argue that there might be good reasons not to trust the media professionals. For example, Michael Ignatieff, leader of the Canadian Liberal Party, did a series of programs on nationalism and terrorism for the BBC in 1993. Ignatieff argued that it was simply impossible to understand those who justified political violence without talking to them. However, the BBC refused him permission to film and broadcast interviews with Loyalist paramilitary terrorists operating in Northern Ireland.

The Western media is often accused of presenting stereotypical images of Muslims, including pictures such as this. Westerners might feel the juxtaposition of burka and cell phone is intended to highlight an apparent contradiction; for Muslims, there is no contradiction.

Chapter 3

How does the media influence us?

The media is an ever-present influence on life in modern societies—something that makes it an easy target for those looking for scapegoats for a host of social ills. In reality, it is hard to gauge precisely the influence the media has on human behavior. The media cannot brainwash all of the people all of the time, but it can be a powerful way of influencing some of the people some of the time.

Media power

The media has often been seen as a highly effective way of controlling people in modern society. In the book *Nineteen Eighty-Four*, published in 1949, George Orwell painted a picture of a society where people's thoughts were controlled with the help of the mass media. One of the most famous cases demonstrating the power of the media is the 1938 radio broadcast by Orson Welles of H. G. Wells's *The War of the Worlds*, a science-fiction story about an alien invasion of earth. The broadcast included a mock news alert. This had the unfortunate effect of convincing many thousands of listeners that a real invasion was occurring, causing chaos across much of the east coast of America.

Thousands of Americans were taken in by Orson Welles, seen here being interviewed by the press after his radio broadcast of H. G. Wells's classic science-fiction story about the invasion of the earth by aliens.

The Columbine High School massacre in 1999 has led to much debate about the effects of violent movies and games. The perpetrators of the Columbine massacre spent many hours playing computer games such as Doom and were fans of the film *Natural Born Killers*.

Are people always so gullible in the hands of the media? Some people argue that they are, and the way in which fashions and catchphrases are quickly taken up can be seen as evidence for this.

Limits of media power

But a moment of reflection should be all it takes to realize that it is easy to exaggerate both the power of the media and the inability of an audience to think independently. People certainly can copy behavior or attitudes they learn from the media, or they can be panicked by a particular report, but they can also be swift to dismiss things that they disagree with. Many psychologists and sociologists studying the effects of the media have concluded that people are influenced by many factors, but these can rarely, if ever, be pinned down to being solely caused by the media.

Expert View

"Contemporary concerns that children are getting out of hand have been shared by adults for the last 2,000 years. In 1993 there were just short of 100 million cinema attendances in the UK plus 77 million video rentals. In the case of video violence, we might well expect that the British public would contain a sufficient number of disturbed individuals to produce a reliable pattern of well-documented cases where such people were influenced by a film to re-enact its plot."

Guy Cumberbatch, formerly of Aston University, UK

How the news is produced

The news stories we read or hear through the media are the result of the work of many different people, not just the reporter or anchor whose name appears on the screen or page. News organizations have teams of reporters and editors working on different stories, making decisions about which are the most interesting, deciding which page a report should go on, or how many minutes a piece can have in a 25-minute program. And reporters find the stories in a host of ways— from official press releases sent out by organizations, by contacting politicians or business leaders they know, or from people who contact a newspaper or TV station because they believe they have been unfairly treated.

Elite news organizations tend to recruit staff from elite social groups, and journalists working for the most prestigious organizations tend to come from the most prestigious universities. Can journalists recruited from the top layers of society truly speak for everyone?

Expert View

"What is selected and presented as news is driven by pictures and their perceptual and iconic power. Negative events with vivid, graphic pictures and an emotional subtext, often presented with journalistic self-promotion, will be chosen to lead today's news."

Judy McGregor, Massey University, New Zealand

Who decides what's news?

Editors and journalists decide which of the many possible stories should have prominence on the news or in a newspaper. Editors and media professionals are said to act as "gatekeepers"—they use their professional judgment to decide what counts as an important news story. In making their decisions, editors have to consider whether or not they think a story will interest their audience.

Many editors, especially those of the popular daily papers or news programs, often want stories that feature interesting personalities or that can be presented simply and dramatically. Another important consideration is how much space and time are available. If a story cannot be told in a few hundred words or in a few short minutes, it is unlikely to be included. All of these factors mean that complex issues have to be reduced to the bare essentials.

Media professionals argue that if they were doing their jobs badly, people would not buy their papers or watch the TV news; news organizations have to respond to public demand or there would be no demand for their products. BBC TV presenter Jeremy Paxman made this argument about the death of Princess Diana in 1997—news editors wanted to move on, but it was public demand that kept the story running day after day.

News is constructed systematically—what seem random, spontaneous items of news have, in fact, been carefully selected. And just like any other product in modern society, news is manufactured.

A big picture and a dramatic and emotional headline: these are some of the key features editors look for in a front-page story. Successful news stories have to rouse the passions of readers, but drama and emotion do not always provide the best route to understanding complex issues.

Advertising

Some critics see advertising as a legal form of trickery. Advertising companies would argue that their business is vital to help make companies profitable and give consumers the choice and quality they want. The media argues that advertising is what enables the public to have high-quality news and entertainment. What is the truth?

Advertisements and brainwashing

In the late 1950s, American writer and social critic Vance Packard helped popularize the idea that advertisers could brainwash consumers by flashing messages at very high speed—invisible to the naked eye—during the course of an advertisement on TV or at the movie theater. The idea of this "subliminal" advertising has been highly controversial, but today many would argue that the scientific evidence supporting it is flawed.

If subliminal advertising is really effective, then it is hard to explain why some people are unaffected and able to criticize advertising. In fact, there is a strong anti-advertising movement at work across the world—Adbusters—which suggests that the advertisers don't have it all their own way.

Adbusters mount protests against the advertising industry, writing subversive messages on billboards. They call their activities "culture jamming" and aim to highlight the contradictions between the images presented by advertisers and the

"Light a Lucky and you'll never miss sweets that make you fat" *Constance Talmadge*

Constance Talmadge,
Charming Motion
Picture Star

INSTEAD of eating between meals ... instead of fattening sweets ... beautiful women keep youthful slenderness these days by smoking Luckies. The smartest and loveliest women of the modern stage take this means of keeping slender ... when others nibble fattening sweets, they light a Lucky!

Lucky Strike is a delightful blend of the world's finest tobaccos. These tobaccos are toasted—a costly extra process which develops and improves the flavor. That's why Luckies are a delightful alternative for fattening sweets. That's why there's real health in Lucky Strike. That's why folks say: "It's good to smoke Luckies."

For years this has been no secret to those men who keep fit and trim. They know that Luckies steady their nerves and do not harm their physical condition. They know that Lucky Strike is the favorite cigarette of many prominent athletes, who must keep in good shape. They respect the opinions of 20,679 physicians who maintain that Luckies are less irritating to the throat than other cigarettes.

A reasonable proportion of sugar in the diet is recommended, but the authorities are overwhelming that too many fattening sweets are harmful and that too many such are eaten by the American people. So, for moderation's sake we say:—

"REACH FOR A LUCKY INSTEAD OF A SWEET."

Constance Talmadge,
Charming Motion
Picture Star

"It's toasted"
No Throat Irritation-No Cough. © 1929. The American Tobacco Co., Manufacturers

Reach for a Lucky instead of a sweet.

Advertising may not work in such a frightening way as some have claimed, but it may work by seducing us. This vintage ad tries to charm the reader into using cigarettes, suggesting by association with a movie star that if we smoke, we may just became a little bit more like a star ourselves.

reality. For example, much of the cheap clothing sold in Western countries is available only because of the use of child labor in developing countries.

Advertising and the media

Perhaps a more serious concern lies with the relationship between the media and advertisers. Advertising provides a large proportion of the revenue for media organizations, giving rise to the concern that the media may fail to turn its critical eye on the activities of large businesses if doing so could threaten their income. Does the relationship between advertisers and media give both industries too much power over our lives?

"As an industry, we must recognize that ad bashing is a threat to capitalism, to a free press, to our basic forms of entertainment, and to the future of our children."

Jack Myers, American Media Council

"When newspapers, magazines, books and television stations are but one arm of a conglomerate there is obvious potential for the conglomerate's myriad financial interests to influence the kind of journalism that is produced. Such pressures range from pushing the magazine arm of the conglomerate to give a favourable review to a movie or sitcom produced by another arm, to pushing an editor not to run a critical story that could hurt a merger in the works, to newspapers being asked to tiptoe around judicial or regulatory bodies that award television licences and review anti-trust complaints."

Canadian journalist and author Naomi Klein, **No Logo**

What's your opinion?

If advertising can be a powerful way to communicate a message, however imperfect, so can anti-advertising. Adbusters, such as this example from Paris, make some consumers reflect on their actions. Is this a threat to capitalism or just a fair and reasonable counterargument? Should communication be only one way?

Chapter 4

Does the media protect our freedom?

Those who argue in favor of press freedom claim that a free press is a vital element in democratic society. Without free speech, it is argued, governments can oppress citizens and muzzle opposition. A free press and media can hold government accountable by continually scrutinizing the actions of political leaders, by questioning them, and by making them justify their actions.

The power of the press

But the emphasis on the need for a free press to hold political leaders accountable can mean that less attention is focused on the responsibilities of the media. Although press freedom is important for democratic societies, it is also important to bear in mind what responsibilities the media has and what rules or principles it should be governed by in its attempts to hold the powerful to account in the eyes of the public.

There is a delicate balance to be struck between a free media and a media that becomes too powerful, abusing the idea of free speech and a free press in order to profit, perhaps financially, or to support the interests of one powerful group over another. In all countries, the media has to abide by the general laws on communication—such as libel, copyright law, and restrictions on publishing

A throng of photographers like this can seem intrusive and threatening. But being subjected to media scrutiny may help to ensure that the famous and the powerful do not abuse their privileges.

Should sources be confidential?

In legal cases involving national security or where it is considered necessary in order to prevent a crime from being committed, courts in most countries will insist that journalists reveal their sources of information. Journalists who refuse to do this can be charged with the offense of contempt of court. In 2005, *New York Times* journalist Judith Miller was jailed for refusing to reveal the identity of a news source. Miller was released after two months when her source agreed to be named.

Judith Miller insisted that the press's privilege of not having to reveal sources is an essential element of a free press. Can we trust the press? If we can't, who will tell us the truth?

Ms. Judith Miller

secret government material—although the nature of these laws varies considerably from country to country. But these laws are not always simple to apply, and editors and journalists can often argue that they are not applicable.

Journalists and their sources

One of the key areas where the conflict between the rights of the free press and the rights of a government clash head-on is when journalists argue that they cannot reveal their information sources for a controversial news story. When journalists obtain information about a controversial topic—such as terrorism—political leaders may argue that the journalist should reveal the source of the information. Journalists, however, argue that in order to do their job properly, sources have to remain anonymous. Journalists taking this view would argue that their job is to reveal the truth, not to support the short-term interests of any politician, whether elected or not.

Public interest and the media

When journalists and media organizations claim to be acting in the public interest, what exactly do they mean? When media professionals use this expression, they are saying that the information they provide will benefit people generally. The British Press Complaints Commission (PCC) in its editorial code gives some examples of the kind of issues that it believes are in the public interest for the media to investigate and publicize. These include exposing crimes, protecting public health and safety, and preventing the public from being misled. The PCC also states that using "clandestine devices," or bugging, is not acceptable and the media should not pay criminals for information that allows them to profit from crime.

But the matter of what the public has a right to know about is a hot topic of debate all over the world. Often the victims of media attention will argue that the press has the power to ruin a person's life and is out of control. Media professionals counter this by

Some people have said that Princess Diana was literally hounded to death by the press after she died in a car accident in Paris in 1997. Her driver was trying to shake off the chasing paparazzi photographers at the time of the crash in an underpass.

Investigative journalists Carl Bernstein and Bob Woodward, shown here being interviewed themselves, played a vital role in exposing the criminal activity of President Richard Nixon in the early 1970s. Their most crucial information came from an informant whose identity they never revealed, although he identified himself in 2005.

saying that press freedom is vital if the activities of the powerful are to be held up to public scrutiny. If the powers of the press are curbed, they claim, the misdeeds of the rich and the powerful will pass by undiscovered, deceiving the public at large.

Codes of practice

Those who argue that the power of the media should be restricted can point to the case in the UK in 2008 when journalists from the *News of the World* newspaper were imprisoned for having illegally listened to the cell phone calls of well-known figures in the hope of finding news stories. There are similar organizations to the PCC in countries all over the world; the media can argue that it is governed by codes of practice. The media can point out that newspapers often publish critical letters and readers' complaints, and in libel cases apologies have to be published. But in the UK, and commonly elsewhere in the world, editorial codes are often only voluntary, and journalists and media organizations cannot be forced to abide by them. Does an overpowerful media gain from interpreting the idea of public interest so loosely that almost anything goes?

Expert View

Summing up in a case in 2002 where businessman Richard Branson tried to sue author Tom Bower for defamation, the British judge, Justice Eady, said:

"In a modern democracy all those who venture into public life, in whatever capacity, must expect to have their motives subjected to scrutiny and discussed. Nor is it realistic today to demand that such debate should be hobbled by the constraints of conventional good manners."

Media Law, *2004*

The media and democracy

The idea of freedom of expression is very old and goes back to ancient Greece. It is also seen as a key element in modern democratic societies. The First Amendment of the US Constitution states that individuals have the right to freedom of expression and prohibits infringements of press freedom, and article 19 of the Universal Declaration of Human Rights, published by the United Nations in 1948, upholds the right to freedom of expression.

The press jostling race car driver Fernando Alonso. The press often claim they are the guardians of our freedom of expression. But how can that justify some media treatment of celebrities: what rights to privacy—if any—should sports, entertainment, and music celebrities have?

Free expression

The idea of freedom of expression goes hand in hand with the idea of a free press. Democratic societies have supported the idea of press freedom, arguing that it is a vital safeguard to ensure the rule of law—the view that the same laws apply to all citizens, regardless of rank. Freedom of expression and a free press mean that anyone can question elected leaders and challenge their opinions. Views cannot be suppressed just because those in power find them inconvenient or offensive. Examples of state-controlled press and propaganda machines in the past—in Nazi Germany, Fascist Italy, and the USSR—as well as in current societies, such as Iran and China, indicate how useful it can be to control the ideas people can think about.

Limitations on press freedom

However, even in democratic societies, which claim to believe in freedom of the press, there are limits to freedom, as Noam Chomsky, professor of linguistics and campaigner for press freedom, has pointed out. Some of these constraints may seem inevitable, such as preventing journalists from publishing defense secrets that would put the security of a country at risk or preventing publication of material that, intentionally or not, will offend certain social groups or incite hatred. Free expression cannot be complete, some would argue, and if rules or restraints are drawn up and applied democratically, then all is well and good. But as Chomsky has argued, even in democratic societies, governments have an interest in ensuring their views dominate. In addition, democratic societies do not in fact give everyone equal access to the airwaves and to newsprint.

Very different interpretations can be given to what appears to be a simple idea–freedom of the press:

"Stalin and Hitler were dictators in favor of freedom of speech only for views they liked. If you're in favor of freedom of speech, that means you're in favor of freedom of speech precisely for views you despise."

Noam Chomsky

" . . . If all records told the same tale–then the lie passed into history and became truth. 'Who controls the past,' ran the Party slogan, 'controls the future: who controls the present, controls the past.'"

George Orwell, **Nineteen Eighty-Four**

What's your opinion?

Some people argue that the Internet has ushered in a new era of democracy, where governments no longer have the power to control information. But the Chinese government has managed to prevent its people from having unrestricted access to the Internet, and use of the web is heavily monitored.

Striking the right balance

In practice, it's easy to find examples from around the world where the media seems to have crossed over the boundary between ensuring that the public is well informed and intruding into areas of people's personal lives or breaking the libel or criminal laws.

But this raises several questions about the nature of the media. First, it shows the difficulty of regulation. Governments and societies have a choice. They can try to enforce strict rules about how the press and media operate—but that can lead to censorship and is easily abused by politicians who want to keep issues secret. Alternatively, as in many democratic countries, a free press can be accepted as being absolutely essential—but then regulating the media will inevitably be difficult without the right to free speech

FORUM

Views on the need for a free press vary greatly:

"Our liberty cannot be guarded but by the freedom of the press, nor that be limited without danger of losing it."

Thomas Jefferson, third president, 1786

"There are laws to protect the freedom of the press's speech, but none that are worth anything to protect the people from the press."

Mark Twain, "License of the Press" speech, 1873

What's your opinion?

Despite winning an election, Burmese democracy campaigner Aung San Suu Kyi has been imprisoned and placed under house arrest for years. Arguably, however, coverage of her case by the world press means that Burma's dictators have had to be restrained in their treatment of the dissident politician.

The case of the Danish newspaper *Jyllands-Posten* raises the question of what limits, if any, should be placed on freedom of expression. In 2005, the newspaper published cartoons of the prophet Muhammad. Around the world, Muslims protested against the irreverent portrayal of Islam and the prophet. Some of the protests turned violent and there were many deaths.

sometimes suffering unnecessarily as a result. That is not to say that abuses by the media must be tolerated, but in that case, regulating the media will be difficult, and at times, it is inevitable that the boundaries of free speech will be blurred.

Second, some people would argue that the freedom of the press has gone too far in many Western democracies. They argue that rules protecting against censorship have been taken advantage of by the unscrupulous, ultimately eroding moral standards by allowing or making possible the publication of pornography, images of violence, websites expressing racist views, and so on.

Freedom or constraint?

Debates about the rights and wrongs of the media can be seen as part of a wider debate between libertarian and authoritarian approaches. In reality, however, most people's views lie somewhere between the extremes of these positions. But in debating where the lines between freedom and constraint should be drawn, remember that when we refer to the "media" we are talking about newspapers and other media organizations that behave with varying standards and that publish or broadcast a wide range of different material. It is also worth remembering that while the freedom of the press is important, some critics argue that the media does more harm than good precisely because it focuses on the wrong kind of stories and asks the wrong kind of questions. Perhaps the media is not always the best judge of what is in the public interest.

Chapter 5

How is the media regulated?

All countries have rules about libel and freedom of speech, and *media regulation* is a term usually used to refer to the way governments ensure that the media sticks to the rules. In many democratic countries, the media is self-regulating—usually an organization is set up to monitor the media in terms of its fair reporting, respect of privacy, and standards of decency. In the UK, the Press Complaints Commission (PCC) and Office of Communications (Ofcom) perform these functions. These organizations are run by committees or boards representing a range of different media interests, including viewers, academic experts, and politicians. Other European countries and Australia, New Zealand and Canada, have similar organizations. In the US, the Federal Communications Commission (FCC) regulates the media.

Expert View

"Under the current system of self-regulation by the press, were Adolf Hitler to be alive today and an opinion columnist, he would experience no legal impediment to publishing whatever statements he chose regarding Jews and homosexuals. He would not do so only for fear of public outcry and an ensuing drop in circulation."

Rachel Morris, Cardiff Law School

"Remember that journalists working anywhere in Britain have observance of the PCC code as a contractual condition of employment. If they flout it, they can be out of a job."

Peter Preston, The Observer, June 26, 2009

Top-down regulation

In authoritarian regimes, the media is regulated in more rigid ways. In China, for example, several state organizations, including the General Administration of Press and Publication (GAPP) and State Administration of Radio, Film, and Television (SARFT), set strict rules on what content can be broadcast and published. The Ministry of Public Security monitors Internet content and investigates fraud, while the Ministry of Industry and Information Technology (MIIT) regulates the communications infrastructure. Although China's state-run

Larry Flynt, publisher of the pornographic magazine *Hustler*, has been involved in the battle against censorship. But media regulation is concerned not just with the content of publications, but also with ensuring that competition among media businesses, the granting of licenses, and so on is fair.

media and its blocking of the Internet dominate the portrayal of the Chinese media in the West, economic expansion is leading to an increasing diversity of media provision, which is hard for the government to control and regulate. The increase in media providers has forced the government to develop new bureaucratic controls, such as the MIIT, formed in 2008.

In Iran, there is a mix of private and state media, with the state controlling broadcasting and a diverse and privately owned press. But the head of the Islamic Republic of Iran Broadcasting (IRIB) is appointed by the supreme leader of Iran, and a council selected by the president, the head of the judiciary, and the Islamic Consultative Assembly oversees the work of the head of the IRIB.

Challenging the system

Despite the work of regulatory bodies in countries with a free press, the criticism is often made that the media is not sufficiently answerable to the public. All countries have laws against libel—the printing or broadcasting of a statement that lowers a person's public reputation. But the media may in some cases be prepared to pay the cost of a court case, and, since hiring a lawyer to fight a libel case is expensive, it is often commented that the libel laws are really effective only for those with deep pockets.

Privacy is also an important matter. Many figures in the public eye resent what they see as media invasion of their privacy, but the media generally argues that such information is in the public interest. They also claim that attempts to create a privacy law are a threat to democracy and would give the powerful a shield to hide behind.

Striking a balance

In many countries, the media provides space for the public's "right to reply"—but these opportunities are controlled by the media and so the concern is that this could lead to mostly trivial contributions being picked. In the many countries where self-regulation is used to monitor the media, it is argued that such a system is preferable to political control since government regulation could easily lead to a weakened media.

Self-regulation is therefore often considered to be an important method of ensuring the freedom

Max Mosley, president of FIA (the governing body for Formula 1 racing), was at the center of a scandal when allegations of his infidelity were published in 2008. Mosley argued such matters were private. Critics said his behavior made public debate about his suitability for the job justifiable.

Breach of privacy

Model Naomi Campbell took a British newspaper, the *Daily Mirror*, to court in 2002, arguing that her privacy had been breached. The *Daily Mirror* argued that since Campbell was a public figure and had publicly denied using drugs, the publication of a story and secret surveillance photographs of her leaving a Narcotics Anonymous session was in the public interest. After an appeal, the British government came down narrowly in favor of Campbell, saying the *Daily Mirror* had not demonstrated a case on the grounds of public interest.

At one stage in the long-running Naomi Campbell case, the judgment was made that the media can report anything that celebrities do in public. Later it was determined that the public do have a right to know if a celebrity's lifestyle or behavior is at odds with his or her public image.

of

the press.

However, a criticism of this system is that it gives the media too much freedom and that abuses are therefore inevitable. Critics see a conflict of interest since the media stands to gain by publishing and broadcasting material that may not be supported by particularly strong evidence, and so the media cannot be expected to, in effect, "police" itself in regard to issues of privacy, defamation (damaging a person's reputation), bias, or taste.

Creating rules that protect the rights of individuals and yet preserve the freedom of the press is a difficult balance to strike, but many believe that at present the rules tend to favor the media over the individual.

The future for regulation

The mass media is in a period of rapid technological change. This is leading to an increase in media providers and the types of content available to consumers all over the world. It is likely that these changes will affect how the media is regulated as governments try to control a rapidly changing industry. One positive aspect of this change is that a broader diversity of views and opinion may become available to more people.

FORUM

Further development of a self-regulating media may be in the cards in Western countries, but is this true of China, a growing world power?

"We felt that by participating there, and making our services more available, even if not to the 100 percent that we ideally would like, that it will be better for Chinese web users because ultimately they would get more information, though not quite all of it."

Sergey Brin, co-founder of Google, justifying the decision to permit the Chinese government to censor the Google search engine results

"To make money, Google has become a servile Pekinese dog wagging its tail at the heels of the Chinese communists."

Guo Quan, open letter to Google, **The Times,** *February 6, 2008*

What's your opinion?

Before 2005, access to Google in China was patchy. Between 2005 and 2010, Google formed a subsidiary providing services to Chinese users. However, Google agreed to comply with the government's censorship laws. Early in 2010, Google announced that it was considering ceasing to provide services under this arrangement.

Sergey Brin, co-founder of Google, was born in the Soviet Union to Jewish parents who experienced discrimination. Brin was brought up in the US and received a PhD in computer science from Stanford. He says he agonized over the decision to let the Chinese government censor search engine results.

However, technical change will also involve economic change, and funding the media is likely to become more difficult. TV, radio, and the press have relied on advertising and some public funding, but when viewers can screen out advertising and watch TV programs on demand, advertising revenues are likely to fall sharply. Some fear that the problem with this is that the need to make a good profit will force media providers to pander to popular taste, producing cheap entertainment and "dumbing down" content in order to attract the largest viewing figures. In democratic societies, politicians will have to balance the need for a competitive media market with the need to ensure that the less profitable but important services, such as high-quality news and current affairs, are not neglected.

Porous borders

Now that people have access to a global media, a major problem looming for the future is how governments will regulate the media and control broadcasts and content coming from outside their own territories. Cultural and political differences over what are acceptable standards of media programs and content, as well as views on privacy and matters of taste, may be hard for countries to agree on.

Democratic societies may be tempted to develop regulatory systems that focus much more on self-regulation since this will be cheaper and easier to do. Authoritarian regimes may want to exercise much greater constraints; but it remains uncertain whether or not they will be able to keep pace with technological advances.

Chapter 6

How is the media changing?

The invention of the Internet and the availability of cheap personal computers are transforming the media. No longer do people have to rely on newspapers and TV and radio bulletins to bring them news and opinions; people can publish their own ideas and news on a blog or website. Is the coming of the "citizen journalist" a sign that the power of the traditional media and the giant corporations that own it will collapse?

Citizen journalism

The term "citizen journalist" has been coined to describe the many ordinary people who report on events in their communities and publish their work on the Internet. The term includes many bloggers, but citizen journalists can also publish their material on a website, on a wiki (editable web page), or on social networking sites such as YouTube, Flickr, or Twitter. For those critical of the power and biases of the traditional media, citizen journalism seems to offer an exciting alternative.

The work of citizen journalists has had an impact on the traditional media, not least in providing news unavailable from other sources. In protests around the world—for example, in Tibet in 2008 and in

Cheap computers for the masses in Shenzhen, China. The affordability of PCs means that just about anyone can publish opinions, news, or anything else and post it on a website or blog. You no longer need an expensive printing press to make your views public.

Expert View

"When the people formerly known as the audience employ the press tools they have in their possession to inform one another, that's citizen journalism."

"Blogs have been called little First Amendment machines. They extend freedom of the press to more actors."

Jay Rosen, New York University, and Arthur L. Carter, Journalism Institute

Thailand and Iran in 2009—pictures and reports were available only because of the work of citizen journalists, and in 2004, citizen journalists were able to provide images of the devastating Indian Ocean tsunami.

For and against

Supporters of citizen journalism argue that it can do much more than supplement the traditional media. Precisely because they are amateurs, citizen journalists can offer fresh viewpoints, challenging the established news agenda of the mainstream media. Citizen journalism enables the public to turn the tables on the media and produce what they want to read, not what others think they should read.

Citizen journalism has not escaped criticism. Critics point out that citizen journalists lack the training of professionals and may often be politically motivated activists. British blogger Guido Fawkes, for example, has been criticized by mainstream political journalists for being a "conspiracy theorist," who sees all politicians as corrupt and who is himself guilty of pretending to be political neutral. Fawkes, though, defends himself by arguing that the public has been let down by a media that has failed to hold politicians to account—something that bloggers and citizen journalists can put right.

Dan Gillmor, founder of Grassroots Media Inc., argues that new technology has enabled citizen journalists to challenge the power of the established media and so has changed the nature of the modern media.

New versus old

The new media—blogs, websites, and social networking sites—does not just offer users a fresh point of view. In contrast to the traditional forms of media, where one organization communicates to a mass audience, the many new-media providers transmit information to many other people—and people can create as well as receive information. It is a two-way, interactive relationship in a sense that the old media could never be. This poses an enormous challenge to traditional media such as newspapers, jokingly called "dead tree journalism," as well as to TV and to radio.

US soldiers in Afghanistan catch up on the news on a laptop. The speed and reach of new technology is providing a stiff challenge to the traditional media. News on the Internet moves much more quickly than print or even TV and reflects a wider range of views.

Changing the news

The traditional media is being challenged, and not just because the new media offers a fresh point of view. Clay Shirky, professor of Interactive Telecommunications at New York University, argues that citizen journalists do more than just provide a new viewpoint: they actually change the definition of what counts as news. Untrained in the profession of old-school journalism, citizen journalists are not concerned with whether a story fits into the criteria required for a news story—newsworthiness—and just write about whatever interests them.

Expert View

"The old bargain of the newspaper—world news lumped in with horoscopes and ads from the pizza parlor—has now ended. The future presented by the Internet is the mass amateurization of publishing and a switch from 'Why publish this?' to 'Why not?'"

Clay Shirky, **Here Comes Everybody,** *2008*

Since there is now a multitude of blogs and citizen-journalist websites, the traditional media often finds itself having to cover issues it previously would have ignored.

News for free?

The new media also presents an economic challenge to the traditional media. Figures from the Audit Bureau of Circulations in the US indicate a steady drop in newspaper sales since the 1990s. People are getting used to accessing information for free on the Internet, and many newspapers that do go online are either free or charge only for certain services. In the UK, for example, the BBC provides a huge website entirely free. And one of London's leading newspapers, the *Evening Standard*, became free in 2009 to boost circulation and attract extra advertising revenue. Television and radio are also losing some of their audience to the Internet and so face a decline in advertising revenues.

> # FOCUS
>
> ## The cost of change
> Out with the old and in with the new has a human fallout that extends far beyond the boardroom and executive high flyers. This became all too true for one anonymous correspondent to the Recovering Journalist blog site, who was concerned that her journalist husband was going through a bad time at work. "They are expected to send layoff notices next week. He's been in the business over 25 years and knows nothing else . . . and has never gone through anything like this. He is our family's only source of income . . ."

Digital sign screens in stores, sports stadiums, and other public places allow advertisers to try to get their message across to consumers who now routinely skip ads on TV. But this shift in habits also means that newspapers and TV stations are finding their revenue base dying at a worryingly fast rate.

The media of the future

The invention of the first printing press with movable type in the 1440s made possible a whole host of social changes that occurred in the centuries that followed. Some experts argue that we are currently living through a communications revolution that will have implications proving to be just as profound in the future.

Some argue that the Internet is bringing new and more democratic forms of communication. But while the Internet brings new possibilities for many, it is not a forum entirely free of constraint. Many bloggers write anonymously, acting as "whistle-blowers" or using anonymity in order to speak more openly. Yet this freedom has been challenged—in the UK, in 2009, a police officer used his blog to criticize his police force and government policies and found himself being disciplined by his employers. When the case came

Expert View

"One of the good things about the Internet is you can put up anything you like, but that also means you can put up any kind of nonsense. There's a kind of an assumption that if somebody wrote it on the Internet, it's true."

Noam Chomsky, academic,
author, and scientist

"I'm not required by *Wikipedia* policy or as a human being behaving ethically to reveal knowledge that I have if I don't choose to do so."

Jimmy Wales, co-founder of **Wikipedia**

Noam Chomsky, professor of linguistics at the Massachusetts Institute of Technology, is a well-known critic of American foreign policy and an advocate of free speech. His book *Manufacturing Consent* argued that the American media purveys subtle propaganda. Will the Internet be any different?

As this picture indicates, applications such as Google Sky Map can be a lot of fun. But people who have found pictures of their homes on Google Maps have raised the possibility that the technology is becoming frighteningly similar to that depicted in George Orwell's *Nineteen Eighty-Four*. Is Big Brother watching you?

to court, the police officer's defense—that his blog published material in the public interest—was rejected by the judge. Similar judgments have been made in the US. So, will journalists continue to be privileged by the law? If they are, then it might seem that they have more freedom of expression than other citizens—a situation that many people would find unacceptable.

More democratic

Attracting the attention of Internet search engines and of the public will not necessarily be a democratic process; what of the views of minorities? Will they be given the space to express themselves but then simply be pushed to the margins of society? Media expert Clay Shirky argues that the greater number of people publishing material, though offering more choices, will not necessarily mean that all publishers get equal amounts of attention—people will inevitably have to be selective about what they choose to read. However, Shirky thinks that the web will be a force for good because it will allow different communities—hobbyists, political groups, neighborhood groups, and so on—to share their ideas and knowledge.

A new dawn

How the media will change in the future, and what will happen to the power of the traditional media, is uncertain. But whatever happens, change will not be caused by technology, but by people using technology.

Glossary

Adbusters An international group founded in 1989 of campaigners highly critical of the media. Many of the causes with which the group is associated poke fun at or are highly critical of the consumerist nature of modern society.

agenda setting The way the media selects certain issues for discussion, necessarily meaning that other issues are neglected.

authoritarianism A belief that supports or favors strict obedience to authority.

bias An unbalanced, partial, or prejudiced view.

blog A chronologically arranged online journal or diary written for public viewing, usually containing the blogger's personal comments on current events.

broadsheet A large-format newspaper. Broadsheets tend to have long, in-depth articles and, as a result, are thought to be more high-status and "serious" newspapers, compared with smaller-format "tabloid" newspapers. Public demand for the more convenient size of the tabloids has meant that more and more broadsheets have adopted the smaller format.

censorship Suppressing the publication of material that is considered inappropriate for publication because it is harmful or challenging in some way.

culture jamming A way of sabotaging advertisements by adding words or images that change or subvert the original meaning of the advertisement.

defamation A form of libel, involving publication of a false statement that might lead to a person's reputation being damaged, or cause others to regard that person with contempt, hatred, or ridicule.

dog whistling A way of hiding a message in a speech or broadcast by using code words that only certain members of the audience will pick up and understand.

dumbing down Simplifying the content of the news or any story, article, or broadcast.

embedded reporter A journalist who is attached to a military unit that is involved in armed conflict.

First Amendment That part of the US Constitution that forbids constraints on freedom of speech and freedom of the press.

freedom of speech The idea that citizens should be free to say what they like, with only minimal legal constraints.

freedom of the press The idea that the press should be free to publish any opinions and information, with only minimal constraints.

gatekeeper In the media, this refers to someone who controls access to the media—for example, an editor or a producer—who decides what to publish and broadcast and what not.

libel The publication of a false statement that will damage a person's reputation.

libertarian A person who believes in maximizing individual freedoms and in minimizing constraints.

Loyalist paramilitary Describes one of the illegal terrorist groups that does not want a united Ireland and wants Northern Ireland to remain a part of the United Kingdom.

news values The shared set of values that journalists use to determine which stories are newsworthy and which are not.

newsworthiness The qualities that make a story worthy of publication or of being broadcast.

press release A statement sent to newspapers, broadcasters, or other interested parties by a company or organization announcing something that it believes is newsworthy.

propaganda Information that is intended to support a particular group, organization, or agenda.

scapegoat A person or organization who is unfairly blamed for something.

self-censorship Censoring one's own work in order to conform to social expectations.

spin The way a news story is presented in order to benefit an organization or public figure or to show an opposition organization or figure in a bad light.

spin doctor A person whose job it is to help politicians and business clients manage their media coverage and public image.

tabloid A small-format newspaper, half the size of broadsheets. Tabloids are generally regarded as being more popular and less "serious" than broadsheets.

totalitarian Describes a political system where there is only one political party and where differences of opinion are not permitted.

whistle-blower A person who reveals misconduct or malpractice in a business or public institution and reports it to the public, usually through the mass media.

Further information

Books
Abercrombie, Nick and Brian Longhurst. *The Penguin Dictionary of Media Studies.* Penguin, 2007.

Adie, Kate. *The Kindness of Strangers*. Headline, 2005.

Brownlee, Les. *The Autobiography of a Pioneering African-American Journalist.* Main Street Press, 2007.

Kovach, Bill and Tom Rosenstiel. *The Elements of Journalism: What Newspeople Should Know and the Public Should Expect.* Three Rivers Press, 2007.

Schlieffer, Bob. *This Just In: What I Couldn't Tell You on TV*. G P Putnam's Sons, 2004.

Websites
https://adbusters.org
   The website of the global network of activists who are highly critical of mainstream media and the advertising industry.

http://www.guardian.co.uk/media/greenslade
   A blog run by Roy Greenslade, journalist and professor of journalism at London's City University. Lots of information on the world of media business and editorial policies.

http://journalism.nyu.edu/pubzone/weblogs/pressthink
   Jay Rosen's blog. Provides a critique of mainstream journalism and champion of citizen journalism.

http://www.media-accountability.org
   A website produced by the Missouri School of Journalism, which contains a very useful international directory of press councils.

http://www.pcc.org.uk
   The website of Britain's Press Complaints Commission. Explains how to complain and how the system in the UK works.

Index

Entries in **bold** are for illustrations.

Adbusters 22–23, **23**
advertising 11, 22–23, 37, **41**
Afghanistan **40**
Al Jazeera **7**
Alonso, Fernando **28**
AOL Time Warner **10**

BBC 10, 17, 41
Bell, Martin 15
Berlusconi, Silvio **11**
Bernstein, Carl **27**
Bewkes, Jeffrey 10
bloggers, blogs 39, 40, 42
Bosnia 15
brainwashing 22–23
Brin, Sergey 36, **37**
Buffet, Marie-George **9**
bugging 26

Campbell, Naomi **35**
censorship 7, 30, 33
China 28, **29**, 32–33, **36**, 37, **38**
Chomsky, Noam 28–29, **42**
"citizen journalists" 38–39, 40–41
codes of practice 27
coffeehouses **8**, 9
Columbine High School massacre **19**
communication, electronic 6, **7**, **41**
"conspiracy theorist" 39

Daily Courant 8, 9
Daily Mirror 35
"dead tree journalism" 40
Diana, Princess 21, **26**
"dog whistle politics" 13

editors 20–21
"embedded reporters" 15
Evening Standard 41

Fawkes, Guido 39
FCC 32
Flynt, Larry **33**
freedom of expression 28, 30–31
freedom of speech 7

GAPP 32
"gatekeepers" 20
Gillmor, Dan **39**
Google **36**, **43**
Gutenberg, Johannes 8

Habermas, Jürgen 9
Hamas **16**

Ignatieff, Michael 17
    Internet 6, 7, **29**, 32, **36**, **38**,
    38–39, **40**, 41, 42
    search engines 36, 43
Iran 28, 33, 38
IRIB 33

journalists 7, **8**, 9, **12**, 14, 16–17, **20**
    25, 27
Jyllands-Posten **31**

laws
    copyright 24–25
    libel 24, 27, 30, 34
Loan, General **15**

mass media 6, 8, 9
McCain, Senator John 13
McLuhan, Marshall **6**, 7
media 6
    control of 7, 28
    criticism of 10–11, 34–35
    and democracy 9, 28
    influence of 19
    ownership 10–11
    power of 12, 19, 24–25, 26–27
    and public interest 21, 35, 43
    regulation 30, 32–33, 36–37
    and wars 14–15
MIIT 32–33
Miller, Judith **25**
Mills, C. Wright 9
Mosley, Max **34**
Murdoch, Rupert 10, 11
Muslim issues **17**, **31**

national security 25

news 20–21, 40–41

News of the World 10, 27
newspapers 6, 8, 9, 11, **21**, 31
    41
Nineteen Eighty-Four 18, 29, 43

Obama, President Barack **12**
Ofcom 32

Packard, Vance 22
Paxman, Jeremy 21
PCC 26, 27, 32
photographers **24**, **26**
politicians **9**, 12–13
press freedom 7, 24–25, 30–31, 35
    limitations on 28–29, 31
printing press 8, 42
privacy, breach of 34–35
propaganda 28, 42
"public opinion" 9

SARFT 32
Shirky, Clay 40, 43
spin doctors 13
Suu Kyi, Aung San **30**

terrorism 16–17, 25
Thailand 38–39
Tibet 38–39
truth 14
tsunami, Indian Ocean 39
Turner, Ted 11

Universal Declaration of Human Rights
    28

Vietnam War **14**, **15**

War of the Worlds, The 8, 18
websites 31, 41
Welles, Orson **18**
"whistle-blowers" 42
Woodward, Bob **27**